THE
WRITE
TIME

How To Find All The Time You
Need To Write A Book

BRANDY M. MILLER

A 40 Day Writer Publication

Elko, NV   *   http://40daywriter.com

40DAY *Writer*

Other Publications By This Writer:

How To Write An Ebook In 40 Days (or Less)

Creating a Character Backstory

Attention: Permissions,
c/o Brandy M. Miller/40 Day Writer
756 Fir St. #1
Elko, NV 89801

ISBN: 0615790879
ISBN-13: 978-0615790879

DEDICATIONS

Dedicated with heartfelt appreciation to the members of my writer's group, Elko County Writers, who inspired me to write this book but especially to Heather Kennison who patiently tested, edited, and gave me feedback on every chapter and to Catherine Higgenbotham whose "yes" was all the encouragement I needed to take action and make it happen.

Table of Contents

ACKNOWLEDGEMENTS

No author ever does anything without the help and support of a great many people. I wish to acknowledge my husband, Randy, whose patience in driving me to every meeting and whose willingness to allow me to invest in writing made it all possible; my son, Eddie, who provides me the inspiration I need to become a mother worthy of the son that he is and the steadfast calm in the midst of the crisis that makes it possible to get through it all; and my mother, Cheryl, who always told me that I could do anything I set my mind on doing.

I also wish to acknowledge my teachers along the way without whom I would not now have enough skills to put this all together; my WorldWide Marriage Encounter family but especially Bill and Theresa Geck, whose generosity to us has born great fruit in so many untold ways; and to my CRHP sisters, who taught me so much about being a woman of God and developing a servant's heart.

INTRODUCTION

Finding time to write requires making changes to your current lifestyle. You will learn to overcome your bad habits and adopt habits that are healthier and will lead to a more productive, peaceful life while reducing stress. If you are wondering whether or not this book is for you, keep reading.

Top 10 Signs You Need Help Making the Most of Your Time:

1) Putting off your dream of writing a book for years

2) You think you "don't have enough time" to write

3) Writing is on a list of 25 things to do in a single day

4) Writing time is stolen from time for important things like sleeping, eating, bathing, exercising, or praying

5) Regularly missing deadlines, failing to meet commitments

6) Feeling ragged, worn out, or stretched thin

7) Saying "yes" to projects even though you already have too much to do.

8) Feeling like something always gets between you and your writing.

9) Constantly apologizing for failing keep commitments you've made.

10) Feeling like your life is out-of-control

If any of this sounds familiar, this is the book for you.

Stop the Insanity

When you've got 25 things or more on your to-do list for a single day, it's time to stop the insanity. Neither you nor the projects you're working on will benefit from this kind of schedule. You cannot give 25 or more projects the time and attention they deserve in a 24 hour day and still take care of your body's essential needs or nurture relationships with your family and friends. It simply won't happen. Your writing will suffer, the quality of the work you produce will suffer, and you will suffer.

Achieve More, Feel Better

The main reason to buy this book is that it will help you to write more and feel better while doing it. It's not about packing more into your day, it's about looking honestly at where you are in your life, at your current priorities and obligations, and seeing where you can make the time you need to finally get the writing done that you've always wanted to do. Believe me, when you finish writing that first book, when you start achieving your goals and seeing your dreams come true, you'll find that it gives you all the energy you need to start really excelling in life

SECTION 1:
FINDING THE WRITE MOTIVATION

1. YOU HAVE ALL THE TIME YOU NEED

When I was a child growing up, there was a frequent refrain heard in my home of "we don't have enough." Those four words defined and limited us. It was a case of plain and simple ingratitude. It also provided a very handy and convenient excuse not to do the things we needed to do in order to improve the circumstances of our lives. If we had a goal but were afraid we couldn't achieve it, we could simply dismiss our lack of effort by saying, "we didn't have enough time". It removed the responsibility from our shoulders by accusing life, the world, and the universe by being unfair and not providing us "enough" of what we needed to do great things.

I am hereby banishing the words "I don't have enough time" from your vocabulary. You are never to speak those words again. You have 24 hours in your day, just like everyone else does. This is the great equalizer between all human beings. What truly sets us apart from one another isn't the amount of time we have, it's what we choose to do with the time we are given. The millionaire does not have more time in his day than the homeless man who lives under a bridge. The two differ wildly in how they spend that time, though. This is perhaps one of the most important lessons you will learn about maximizing your time.

Take Responsibility for Your Time

I once worked with a woman who was constantly running late. When you asked her why she was late, her answer was inevitably, "Traffic". Without realizing it, she had subconsciously allocated herself the role of victim to this monster known as traffic. Since she was busy blaming traffic for her problems, she was unable to see where she was contributing to the problem and because she viewed the problem as being outside of her control, she wasn't able to see how she might help solve the problem. Those solutions might have been as simple as leaving 5 minutes earlier each morning, or trying different routes, or even asking someone else who was on time every day how they did it and seeing if she could implement that advice. She'll never know, though, because she sees it as a problem outside of her control and so she isn't seeking solutions.

When you take personal responsibility for how your time gets spent instead of blaming your circumstances, you free yourself to find solutions to your problem of finding time to write. Blaming your circumstances may have been easier for you because it didn't require you to change anything or make real efforts to accomplish anything, but it doesn't actually help you to write more or to find solutions to your problems. Put simply, whatever or whoever you blame for your problems owns your successes as well. You want to take full credit for any writing success you experience, so you're going to have to take full ownership of your time management skills as well.

Change Your Attitude

Taking responsibility for your time begins with changing your attitude about time. It's not outside of your control. As of this point forward, when you are tempted to say, "I don't have enough time" instead, you are going to say to yourself, "I have all the time I need. How can I get this done?" This simple change in the way you look at your time will help you open yourself up to solutions you didn't even think of before and will eventually lead you to a life that doesn't feel so out-of-control.

EXERCISES

Step 1. What are things you have wanted to do with your life, but have told yourself you couldn't because you didn't have enough time?

_____

_____

_____

_____

_____

_____

_____

_____

_____

_____

_____

Step 2. Look at your list. Which of these things do you truly want to accomplish? Put a star by those.

BRANDY M. MILLER

2. KNOW WHAT YOU WANT

Life is a journey, but unless you know where you want to go, that journey can end up being meandering, fruitless, and potentially perilous to your health and safety. Knowing what you want does not always guarantee a safe or swift journey, but it does make it easier to plan and to avoid hazards. For instance, if you simply hop in your car and drive without having a destination in mind, you are likely to encounter road construction that you didn't anticipate and could even run out of gas in a spot where there's no gas station for miles around.

I know a man who did that once, and ended up having two men relieve him of his wallet at gunpoint while he was stranded by the side of the road! Needless to say, it is best to know where you are going so that you can plan your route ahead of time and reach your destination with as little stress as possible.

Reaching Your Destination

If you've purchased this book, it is because you want to be a writer or at least write a book. Many thousands of people in this world aspire to be writers also. The main difference between them and you is that the desire to reach their destination isn't strong enough for them to actually make consistent, persistent daily effort toward it. Your brain is a muscle, and writing requires you to use that muscle frequently whether through imagination, research, putting together the right wording, or simply brainstorming ideas.

Consistent, Persistent Effort

Like any muscle, your brain needs regular workouts for it to be at peak condition, ready and able to deliver when and where you need it. You wouldn't attempt to run a marathon and expect to be successful if you hadn't spent months before hand getting your muscles into the shape where they could support that kind

25

of run, and you shouldn't expect to produce a book – the intellectual equivalent of a marathon – without putting in that same time getting your intellectual muscle in shape.

This is why learning to make effective use of your time is so important to the success of your writing. It ensures that you schedule the time into your life that will allow you to put in the consistent, persistent effort toward you goal that keeps your brain working like a fine tuned engine.

Shoot for the Stars

If you are like some people I know, it may be hard for you to believe that you can be a success. Believing that you can accomplish your dreams, that you can publish a book, may be harder for some people to hold onto than others. For you, I want you to shoot for the stars. If you set your sights high, you may not reach your goal – but would you really complain if you got close?

What if you set your sights on finishing a book in one year, but it takes you two years instead – is that really so bad? At least you will have made the effort and you'll know that you can do even better the next time! I guarantee you can finish a book. I know that no matter who you are and no matter how badly you may have failed before, you can do better. That's why I'm here – to help you succeed.

EXERCISES

Step 1. Decide on your destination. What do you want to accomplish? Are you aiming for one book? For a career as a writer? Write down what it is you want.

_____

_____

_____

_____

_____

_____

_____

_____

_____

_____

_____

_____

_____

_____

Step 2. For each goal you have, write down what it would mean to you if you were to accomplish that goal.

_____

_____

_____

_____

_____

_____

_____

_____

_____

_____

_____

_____

_____

_____

_____

3. KNOW WHY YOU WANT IT

On any journey you undertake, you are bound to wind up encountering obstacles, setbacks, and problems which will have to be overcome if you are to reach your destination. The same thing is true about your writing. If writing is only a vague notion of something you'd like to do, but isn't really important to you, that's how you'll treat it. You'll push it to the back burner and allow it to eventually drop off your to-do list altogether. If, however, you have a burning desire to write and know why it really matters to you to get your book written, then you'll have the internal motivation you need to push past those obstacles, overcome the setbacks, and find solutions to your problems so that you can continue writing.

A Worthy Desire

You may be writing because you're hoping to overcome a financial hurdle, and that's a good enough reason to get started. However, it probably won't be enough to keep you going when you're tired and you don't feel like writing. Dig deeper. What would being a successful writer mean to you? What would it mean to your family? What would you be able to do for your children if you were to become successful as a writer? You need a reason that's strong enough and worthy enough to keep you writing even when your world turns completely upside down — because when you set out to succeed at anything, you can virtually guarantee that everything in your life WILL turn upside down.

Visualize Success

Take the time to create an image in your mind of what success will look like for you. What will you do? Where will you go? Make this so real you can practically taste it. Use a bulletin board (Pinterest works nicely for this purpose if you don't have an actual bulletin board) and pin images of the life you will lead when you are successful. If you're hoping to use the money from your book to move your kids to a nicer neighborhood, or maybe buy a home, start picking out the home you want and pin it to the board. Make success so real that you can practically taste it, and every time you get discouraged go and stare at that board and remind yourself of why you are writing in the first place.

EXERCISES

Step 1. Write a paragraph about why you really want to write. Be specific.

_____

_____

_____

_____

_____

_____

_____

_____

_____

Step 2. Create the "why" bulletin board.

Step 3. For each item on that board, write about what it would mean to you to achieve that dream.

_____

_____

_____

_____

_____

_____

_____

_____

_____

_____

_____

_____

_____

_____

_____

_____

BRANDY M. MILLER

4. KNOW WHEN YOU WANT IT

Now that you know what you want, it is time to determine when you want these things to happen. How long do you want it to take to have a finished manuscript in hand, ready for the editing? How long do you want it to take for you to achieve your dreams and goals? The future is in your hands – and this is the point where you begin to decide for yourself how long that journey will be.

Daily, Monthly, Weekly, Yearly

While you cannot control everything that happens to you, you have every ounce of control over what you choose to do about it. Your choices today largely determine where you will end up tomorrow, in a month from now, in a year from now, in five years from now. So it's important to set your goals based on where you want to be, rather than allowing yourself to drift along through life in the hopes that you'll somehow miraculously end up where you dream of being, because without direction that's all you do – drift.

Take some time today to decide where you want to be in five years from now. Do you want to be on the path to a successful writing career? Where do you want to be in 2 years from now? In one year? In six months? In 3 months? A month from today? Two weeks from now? A week from today? Once you know where you want to be and when, it makes it easier to create the checkpoints that will ensure you're making steady progress toward achieving your goals.

Determining Check Points

When you plan out a journey from your home town to a faraway city, you likely grab your atlas, your map, or look up the directions on the internet and begin looking at the stops you'll be making along the way. You plan your driving to allow time to stretch your legs, grab something to eat, and decide whether you need to stop and sleep along the way. You also note the towns that you'll be passing through so you know that you're on the right path.

You need to do this same kind of thing for your writing. If, for example, you want to write a 100,000 word novel in a year's time, that's going to require you to write 8,334 words per month. That's 2,084 words per week, and 298 words per day. 298 words is roughly a page of double spaced type-written words. That's an incredibly simple goal, and one you can easily achieve with a little bit of effort.

EXERCISES

Step 1. Write down your 5 year, 2 year, 1 year, 6 month, 3 month, 1 month, 2 week, 1 week, and daily goals.

_____

_____

_____

_____

_____

_____

_____

_____

_____

_____

_____

_____

_____

_____

_____

Step 2. For each goal you have set, break down what it will take to achieve those goals. Create an action plan for achieving each of those goals. What is the price for failure? What is the reward for success?

_____

_____

_____

_____

_____

_____

_____

_____

SECTION 2:

LIVING THE WRITE LIFE

5. KEEP A TIME JOURNAL

Becoming aware of how you currently spend your time will help you to more effectively learn to manage it. For the next 60 days, you are going to keep a time journal. Bring it with you everywhere you go, even to work. You can make a time journal yourself out of a notebook, or you can buy the journal that goes with this book, either is fine. Every time you do something during the day, note when you begin the activity and when you end it.

This includes the more personal activities such as brushing your teeth, even going to the bathroom. If you are uncomfortable with that, worrying that someone might read your journal, create a code for yourself that notates the type of activity it is. If you like, you can use your smart phone to keep track of these things. It doesn't matter how you do it, what matters is that you do it.

Graph your time

At the end of each day, graph the amount of time you spend on each type of activity you do. Ideally, plug the information into a spreadsheet. This will help you begin to detect patterns of behavior, times where you are actually wasting time that could be better spent elsewhere, and give you a more realistic idea of how you really spend your time. In turn, you'll begin to see just how much free time you really have to devote to writing or other activities. Best of all, when you're tempted to overbook yourself by saying yes to something you'd rather say no to, you can rest secure that you really don't have room to add this activity to your schedule.

The Results Become Clearer Over Time

This is one aspect of effective time management that cannot be rushed. You need at least a month, and preferably two, before you really begin to see the patterns that will form in your life which affect your productivity. I will quote from a man by the name of Trent Hamm on his blog The Simple Dollar in which he discovered the benefits of keeping a time journal or diary:

"Simply put, the entire purpose of a time diary is to figure out simple things you can change that make a big impact on your day-to-day life. I learned how much of an impact spending a couple hours cleaning my office can really have. I learned how direct the positive impact of reading is on my life. I learned that going to bed around ten during the school week is probably optimal.

These little things make a huge difference in my weekly productivity. They seem like small tweaks, but the impact of these tweaks is felt during every hour of every day in the form of increased energy and alertness and mental productivity. This adds up to more income and more life enjoyment as well. Those types of discoveries are well worth the time that such a task takes up. It really can change your life in a positive way."

My Experience

When I began keeping a time journal, just the first day was an eye-opening experience. I realized that Facebook is one of my biggest distractions and I need to close it out completely when I am trying to work on a project. I also realized that when my blood sugar drops because I have gone too long without eating, I am more easily distracted than normal and have a very hard time focusing. These two insights alone were worth the hassle of trying to track my every move.

EXERCISES

Step 1. Decide how you are going to journal your time.

Step 2. Begin recording your time right now!

_____

_____

_____

_____

_____

_____

_____

_____

_____

_____

_____

_____

_____

_____

_____

BRANDY M. MILLER

6. YOUR BIGGEST PRIORITIES

A college professor walked into class one day carrying two jars, two large rocks, two bags of pebbles, and two bags of sand. Without saying a word, he set all of this on his desk. When the time came for class to begin, he put one of the large rocks inside of the jar. "The large rock," he said, "represents the big priorities in your life, the ones that are the reason you do everything else you do. It represents your family, your children, your spouse, and your friends."

He then took the pebbles and dumped them in the jar. "The pebbles represent the things you have to do to be able to support your big priorities in life – such as work, school, studies, paying bills, etc."

He then took the sand and dumped it in the jar. "The sand represents everything else you do with your time. Notice that everything fits."

He took that jar and set it to the side. He then took the empty jar and put the sand in first, then the pebbles, and tried to fit the big rock inside. No matter how he tried, the large rock simply wouldn't fit.

"This is how life works. If you put the important things – your relationships with your family, friends, spouse, and children – first, everything else will flow around those and you will have plenty of time for them all. If, however, you live your life in the wrong order, nothing really fits. The choice is up to you. Choose wisely."

Making the Most of Your Time

Making the most of your time isn't about cramming more things into your life. It's about recognizing what matters most to you and spending your time only on those things that support your biggest priorities. This is why it's so important to really look at what does matter to you before worrying about scheduling your time. You may be engaging in lots of activities that don't really support your main priorities or help you to live your life with integrity.

Living a Life of Integrity

It is important to live our lives with integrity. What I mean by this is that what we say our priorities are should be reflected in what we do with our time, how we spend our money, how we treat others, and in what we are willing to sacrifice to accomplish our goals. You can lie to yourself, you can lie to others, but when it comes to your writing you cannot successfully lie to your audience. Who you really are and what you truly value will inevitably reveal itself in your writing, so keep this in mind.

What are your biggest priorities?

If you want to know what your biggest priorities in life are right now, keep track of where you spend the majority of your free time and your money. Do you spend most of it playing video games? Then, video gaming is your biggest priority. Do you spend most of it working? Then work is your biggest priority. If this is truly how you want to live your life, then don't change what you're doing. However, if you take a look at where you spend your time and decide that you aren't happy with what it's telling you about what your priorities really are, now is a great time to change those priorities.

I will give you a hint: Your job will not be at your bedside when you are dying, holding your hand. You might be lucky to get a bouquet of flowers from them, if they remember you at all. Your video game will not be there when you are sick, either. Your high score will not come visit you in the nursing home. No book you write, no matter how grand it might be, will do this for you either. Your biggest priorities in life should be the relationships you form with other people and, if you are a person of faith as I am, with your God. These are the things that will give you lasting happiness and joy.

EXERCISES

Step 1. Ask someone who lives with you for their perspective on what your priorities are right now. If you live alone, this will be more difficult, but examine where you spent most of your free time over the last week. Where do you spend most of your money? These two things will tell you a lot about what your priorities really are. Are you happy with this answer?

_____

_____

_____

_____

_____

_____

_____

_____

_____

Step 2. If you are happy with this answer, write one sentence describing each of your top three priorities. Then write a

45

paragraph describing why these priorities really matter to you. What would your life be like without them? How has your life changed because of these priorities? If you aren't happy with the answer, choose three new priorities. Why do these new priorities really matter to you? What would your life be like if you lost them because you didn't give them the attention they needed?

_____

_____

_____

_____

_____

_____

_____

_____

_____

_____

_____

_____

_____

_____

7. YOUR SECONDARY PRIORITIES

Your secondary priorities are the things you do that are important to you and you wouldn't want to stop doing them, but if absolutely necessary you would sacrifice them for the sake of your biggest priorities. Writing, for example, is most likely one of these secondary priorities in your life.

Your job – whether you enjoy it or not – is probably also a secondary priority since you need it to support yourself and your family. The trick is to make sure that your secondary priorities help support your biggest priorities and eliminate or reduce those that don't.

Secondary Priorities and Time

Oddly enough, we usually spend a majority of our time on our secondary priorities in life. For example, although family may be one of my biggest priorities in life, I may spend 8 of my 16 waking hours each day working, 1 hour getting ready for work, and 1 hour on transportation to and from work. This may leave me very little time to actually spend with my husband and son. This is why it is important to evaluate our secondary priorities in terms of how well they align with our primary priorities and eliminate as many conflicts as possible.

Secondary and Primary Priority Conflicts

If you completed the exercise in chapter three, you may have discovered that you actually have a conflict of priorities. One or more of the three big priorities you choose may be in direct conflict with one of your secondary priorities. For example, your job may require you to spend more time away from your family than you spend with it.

When this happens, it isn't time to panic but it is time to start looking for an opportunity to change your secondary priority. In the case of a job, look at your life and figure out what expenses you could eliminate so that you can afford to take a job closer to home even if that job isn't as financially lucrative as the one you hold now. Doing this may also free up more of your time to follow your passions, such as writing!

Harmonious Living

When your primary and secondary priorities are in harmony with one another, when there is a balance between them, your life will begin to be less stressful. You will find that you feel less tense, your quality of free time improves because you can really enjoy it without feeling the strain of constant guilty feelings, and your relationships with others improve as well because you are giving them the time and attention they need to grow.

EXERCISES

Step 1. Identify your secondary priorities. Where do you spend most of your day? How much time each day do you spend on these secondary priorities currently? Are these secondary priorities in line with your primary priorities? Are there any that can be eliminated or that need to be changed?

_____

_____

_____

_____

_____

_____

_____

_____

_____

_____

_____

_____

_____

_____

Step 2. What steps can you take to bring your secondary priorities in line with your primary priorities? What sacrifices will this require? What improvements to your life will it bring if you make these changes? Create an action plan to make the necessary changes in your life.

_____

_____

_____

_____

_____

_____

_____

8. YOUR EXISTING COMMITMENTS

Whether it's a Friday night poker session with the guys, a Saturday morning coffee meeting with the ladies, or committee meetings with a local club, the chances are high that you already have commitments you've made to other people which are taking up some of your time. It is possible that some of these commitments may need to be re-evaluated, reduced, or even eliminated because they no longer fit in with the priorities you have chosen for your life.

Evaluating Existing Commitments

Commitments are an important part of forming relationships. Relationships, as I stated in chapter six, should be at the center of your biggest priorities because they are the things that will bring you lasting joy and happiness. Therefore, if you have existing commitments. you must be careful about breaking them because of the damage it is likely to do to relationships. The only exception to this rule is when the commitment you've made is not a good one for either of you.

As a rather extreme example, a crack addict may have an existing commitment every day at 3 p.m. with his or her crack dealer, but this is not a relationship that truly benefits either of them and therefore this commitment should be eliminated altogether. The Friday evening poker sessions, by contrast, form bonds of friendship and so this existing commitment is one that might need to be reduced since it could be taking away time from the family but it probably shouldn't be eliminated since it is helping to foster friendships.

Mapping Out Your Commitments

Making the most of your time requires you to know where your time is allocated, so it's important to write down each commitment you have, when you are required to be there, and how long it takes you for each day of the week. This allows you to begin the task of pinpointing exactly how much time you have available for each day of the week to allocate to your writing.

Handling Over-Commitment

Some people have a harder time setting boundaries and saying "no" than other people do. People who have a hard time setting boundaries can easily find themselves with more commitments on their time than they can reasonably fulfill. This leads to stress, guilty feelings, and the constant feeling of not having enough time. While it may seem "nice" to say yes when you'd rather say no, the truth is that saying yes when you probably shouldn't only leads to disappointing those people because you will never perform your best when you can't give it your full attention. If, after running through the list of commitments and the times they are required to be done, you discover that two or more of your commitments overlap, it is time to begin pruning back.

Begin with the commitments that are in direct violation of your biggest priorities – those things that lead you away from what matters most to you. Move to the commitments that give you the least return on the investment of time that you are making. For example, if there are two activities of equal value, but one of them helps you build higher quality relationships than the other one does, choose the one that build higher quality relationships.

52

EXERCISES

Step 1. Map out your commitments. Do any of these commitments cause conflict between your stated priorities?

_____

_____

_____

_____

_____

_____

_____

_____

_____

_____

_____

_____

_____

_____

_____

Step 2. Write out an action plan to reduce or eliminate those commitments that you have made which conflict with your stated priorities. Include answers to these questions: How much time will you gain by eliminating or reducing these commitments? How will this help you succeed in your writing goal?

_____

_____

_____

_____

_____

_____

_____

_____

_____

_____

_____

_____

_____

SECTION 3:
CREATING THE WRITE PLAN

9. THE FIVE NON-NEGOTIABLES

Sleeping, eating, exercising, hygiene, and praying/meditating are the five non-negotiables of any healthy life. These are called non-negotiables because under no circumstances should they be eliminated from your life, nor should you skimp on the time you spend doing these things.

Sleep and the Creative Process:

While you are awake, the brain gathers all of the information you receive through your senses and attempts to file it by its relationship to things you already know. If the brain isn't able to find a relationship between the bit of information you received and something you already know, it tosses it in the rough equivalent of a mental "junk" drawer to be sorted out while you are dreaming.

This is why sleep, especially sleep that reaches the REM state of dreaming, is so important. It is during dreams that the brain rummages through the contents of that junk drawer and tries to make connections between what's in that drawer and the stuff that's already filed away. This is why so many writers experience incredible breakthroughs and insights during dream states.

Furthermore, if the brain doesn't get enough rest at night, it has a hard time doing its job of processing information the next day and is likely to miss important connections. Things that should get connected end up being tossed into the junk drawer by accident, with a possibility that they might never be connected to anything of significance. This is another reason why sleep is so important to writing.

57

Proper Nutrition and the Writer:

Writing takes quite a toll your mental faculties because it's a highly creative process that taps into many areas of the brain. Like any muscle, the brain needs fuel to keep working at that high level, so proper nutrition is just as important to the brain as sleep. Getting enough to eat, making sure that what you eat is healthy for you, and drinking plenty of water are all important parts of keeping your brain functioning at this high level for as long as possible so you can keep writing.

As I stated in chapter five when I talked about keeping a time journal, I personally experienced what happened to my ability to concentrate when I neglected eating regularly. The time taken to prepare a meal may seem like wasted time, but in reality it would have saved me time because I was having such a hard time concentrating that I was even more distracted than I normally am.

Exercise for Better Writing

Exercise releases endorphins in the brain that will help to keep you awake and alert, make you feel better about yourself, and ensure that the brain receives enough oxygen. It also helps to boost your immune system and keep you healthier so you can write longer more often. Furthermore, while the brain does require some fat in order to produce the myelin sheathes that keep your brain's neurons firing correctly, too much fat can thicken those sheathes to the point where they actually slow down neural transmissions. So, don't compromise when it comes to exercise.

Prayer/Meditation and Creating Negative Space

When I was studying art at the college level, our instructor began teaching us about the importance of negative space. In art, the negative space is the open space where nothing is happening. It is important because that negative space allows the eyes to be drawn to the action areas of the canvas and define those more clearly. Think about a toddler's first drawing – it's nothing but a chaotic blob of scribbles.

It's only when you start to add some negative space between things that you can clearly define the individual elements. The same thing is true about your writing and your life. The time you take to build negative space into your life will help define and shape you. You may not believe in God, but that doesn't mean you can't benefit from 30 minutes of meditation. You will experience a calmer and more peaceful life if you include it, and that calm and peace is something that benefits every writer.

Proper Hygiene Makes for a Happier Writer

I probably shouldn't have to say this, but it's important. Proper hygiene for the writer is a non-negotiable. Keep your hair combed, your body washed, and your teeth clean. Not only will this make you feel better, it will also help to keep you healthy. It's hard to concentrate when you've got a tooth ache caused by a failure to brush often enough. Plus, the break you take to shower or brush your teeth can create the room needed for the brain to develop new ideas.

EXERCISES

Step 1. How much time are you currently spending each day doing these things?

_____

_____

_____

_____

_____

_____

_____

Step 2. How much time should you be giving to these things each day?

_____

_____

_____

_____

_____

_____

_____

Step 3. Write out an action plan to improve where you need it.

_____

_____

_____

_____

_____

_____

_____

_____

_____

_____

_____

_____

_____

_____

_____

_____

10. BLOCKING YOUR TIME

Every day can be broken in to twelve two-hour time blocks. Finding more time for your writing begins by look at each day and blocking out those time segments that are already taken up with your biggest priorities, secondary priorities, existing commitments, and non-negotiables. Look at what's left and see where writing fits in to each day.

One Month at a Time

Before beginning to block your time, open up a calendar program or grab an old-fashioned printed monthly calendar and divide each day into the twelve blocks. Then start filling them in with pencil at this point, since later on you'll be making changes.

The Non-Negotiables

Sleep should be done in four continuous blocks. Eating and hygiene will take up one block. Exercise and prayer or meditation should take a half block. This means five and a half blocks of your twelve are taken up with the non-negotiables. This leaves you six and a half blocks for everything else you need to get done in a day.

Commute Time

How much time do you spend commuting back and forth to work each day? Is it ½ block? 1 full block? Don't worry if this isn't the same every day because of traffic. Try to guestimate an average amount of time and add that to your blocks for every day that you go to work or travel to school.

Work or School Time

How much time do you spend working or going to school? Is it a full-time, part-time, or some time affair? What days of the week do you go? Is it every day? Every other day? What are your days off?

Existing Commitments

What pre-existing commitments do you have outside of work? How much time per day do you spend on these commitments? Are they a once-a-month, once-a-week, or once-a-day commitment? Block out time for this commitment based on that information.

Family/Friends

Look at the open time blocks. Make sure that at least once a week, more often if possible, you assign a block of time to spend with friends or family. If you have underage children at home with you, plan on a block of time for family per day.

Writing Time

What blocks are left after all of the other things have been arranged? How many of these blocks can you assign to your writing?

No Time?

If you've combed over your time and you can't find a space for writing, don't worry. We're about to examine ways that you can work toward finding the time you need to write while still taking care of everything else, including your friends and family.

EXERCISES

Step 1. Now that you've spent the time actively arranging your schedule on paper, take a moment to evaluate how you feel. Angry? Sad? Overwhelmed? Happy? Excited?

_____

_____

_____

_____

_____

Step 2. Write a paragraph about how your current schedule makes you feel. Do you want to change anything?

_____

_____

_____

_____

_____

_____

_____

BRANDY M. MILLER

11. COMBINING ACTIVITIES

In order to give yourself all the time that you need without eliminating the important things or short changing yourself of any of the big five non-negotiables, you may need to look at what activities you can do that can be combined with other activities. In my own life, in order to find the time to exercise, I usually pray while I exercise. The walk helps me to clear my mind so I can focus. I get the quiet and alone time that I need to really think, and my body benefits as well If your chosen method of connecting is meditation, you may not be able to combine it with exercise, so you'll have to look in other places to find activities you can combine.

Meals and Writing

I wouldn't recommend doing this for every meal, but you may be able to combine your lunch or breakfast time with your writing time, especially if you tend to eat at work anyway. Be sure to bring foods that are easily consumed with one hand and aren't too messy, otherwise you'll risk getting your food places you don't want it to be. This can be a great way to grab some writing time without sacrificing the body's need for good nutrition.

Commute Time and Writing

If you purchase an audio recorder and store it in the car, your commute time can become a perfect time to "write" out your story by working out scenes and dialogue audibly. This has an added advantage of letting you hear how the dialogue sounds before you've written it, so you can get it just right when it's time to commit it all to paper. Bring the recording to your next writing appointment and play it as you type it up. You'd be surprised at how much you can get done this way, without distracting you too much from your focus on the road. (I do

NOT recommend writing while driving. Nobody benefits from a dead author).

Another way to combine your commute time and writing is to see if you can't take public transportation of some sort or car pool with someone else to work. While you are travelling you can then write to your heart's content as you head to work, allowing you to get more done and freeing up time for your family without sacrificing your dreams.

Exercise Time and Writing

Just as you can with your commute, you can spend your exercise time audibly working out scenes so that when you do have time to sit down with pen and paper or put fingers to keyboard, you already know most of what you want to say and are just transcribing the audio file.

Bathroom Breaks and Writing

Bathroom breaks usually last between 4-5 minutes, which is time that you can spend writing. Even if you only manage to write 25 words each break, over the course of an entire day you can put yourself 100 words closer to your goal every day that you do this. If you don't have a laptop or other mobile device to use, bring a small notepad and pen with you when you go.

EXERCISES

Step 1. After looking over your time blocks, identify time blocks that could be combined together to achieve more.

_____

_____

_____

Step 2. How much time will you gain by combining these tasks? What sacrifices might you have to make in order to make this possible? Is what you are gaining worth the cost?

_____

_____

_____

_____

Step 3. Do you need any tools or equipment to make it possible for you to combine these blocks?

_____

_____

_____

_____

_____

_____

_____

12. LETTING GO

In chapter 8, we spent a little time discussing the need to eliminate commitments that conflict with your overall goals. However, in all likelihood that's not the only area of your life where you are spending time that you can re-allocate to other things. If you're going to find the time you need to write, you're going to have to make room for it by giving up things you'd like to do but that are not really necessary.

TV

Almost everyone in America spends way too much time in front of a television set. I'm not going to tell you what to do on this one, but consider that if you eliminate just one television program that lasts an hour each week from your routine, you have found an hour of time for your writing. You need to decide what matters most: the television or the writing goal. If you're having trouble deciding, I will just say that there are few things in life that beat the feeling of accomplishment that comes when you have finished your first 50,000 word novel or non-fiction book and you know that you can do it.

Video Games

There are video games that can actually stimulate your creativity, such as simulation RPG's like the SIMS Franchise, but most of them are just massive time wasters that will eat up minutes, hours, and whole days that you could have been using to write your novel. I'm not saying you need to give them up forever, but you do need to be aware of the trade you are making. Every hour you spend playing your video game is one hour you aren't spending on achieving your goal. It's also one hour that you could be putting in to get closer to that goal.

Social Media

While developing a social media presence is an important part of creating a marketing campaign and it does require that you spend a certain amount of time on your accounts each day in order to develop the relationships and trust that you need to build a following, the total amount of time you spend on social media really should not be more than one hour a day, and less than that if possible.

If you have little free time, save your social media time for posting about your book progress and link your Facebook and Twitter accounts so that the updates go from Twitter directly to your Facebook feed. Make a couple of comments on your friends/family/fan pages, and then get off and go write!

Shopping

My own family has a bad habit of not planning out our shopping trips ahead of time. As a result, we end up wasting time and gas making multiple trips to the stores to get this or that. We also sometimes head to the store with a purpose but then take time to "window shop", wandering aimlessly for hours as we look at all the stuff that's available. This is a huge waste of time and can be eliminated by planning your shopping trips ahead of time so that you know exactly what you are going to buy before you get there, and then leaving as soon as you find what's on the list.

EXERCISES

Step 1. After looking over your time journal, where have you been spending time that could be better spent writing? How much time would you gain just by eliminating these activities?

_____

_____

_____

_____

_____

_____

Step 2. Write an action plan to let go of what you can afford to eliminate from your schedule.

_____

_____

_____

_____

_____

_____

_____

_____

_____

SECTION 4:

TAKING THE WRITE ACTION

13. MAKE AN APPOINTMENT

It's easy to procrastinate, to promise yourself you'll do your writing some day at some undefinable point in the future when everything is going well and you have "more" time than you do now to get it done. The problem is, this day never comes. There's always going to be something in your life that will take your time and attention away from your writing and push your dream of becoming a writer back down to the bottom of the pile. The only way you will ever combat this is to set an appointment with yourself.

Now that you have reworked your calendar to free up some additional time for writing, it's time to set that appointment for your writing time. The amount of time you need to set aside for writing depends upon when you want your book to be finished, as discussed in chapter four. For example, if you want the book written in three years, you need to find time to write 100 words. It should take you roughly 10 minutes to write such a small amount. However, if you are trying to write 1100 words (putting you on a schedule to complete a 100,000 word book in 91 days), you'll need to allow yourself roughly two hours for that, or one entire block.

Take It Seriously

Write it down, make it a date, and create an event on your Facebook calendar or your Google calendar or your Outlook account. Put it into your iPhone or iPad. Set a reminder for yourself, and then keep it. If you set a two hour appointment with yourself once a week and manage to write only 975 words during that time, over the course of two years you will have a novel of 100,000 words ready. If you do this twice a week, you can finish a novel in a year's time. If you do this three times a week, it will take you only 33 weeks (just a little more than eight months). If you do it four times a week, it will take you only six months. You get the idea.

No Interruptions, No Distractions

Your appointment time must be done some place where you will have no interruptions and no distractions. Treat it as you would if you were meeting an important person, because you are! Turn off the cell phone, turn off the home phone, turn off the television and disconnect from the internet. You want to focus every ounce of your energy on writing, and anything else will just get in the way.

If you have young children, hire a sitter or trade sitting with another mother so that you can have the time away from your kids. If you have a spouse, make sure they understand this is important to you and you are not to be interrupted. If they just can't get the message through their heads, go to a nearby coffee shop, restaurant, library, or even your car with your laptop or note pad. Write until you have reached the end of the two hours, even if that means you write more than you expected to write.

Pack Supplies Ahead of Time

Prepare for your writing appointment in the same way that you would any other appointment. Pack your supplies ahead of time. Create a check list to be sure everything you need to write effectively is at your fingertips and readily available. Make a binder for yourself that contains all your notes on your characters, the progress you've made, the ideas you've had since your last appointment, and anything else you might need to know. Create or purchase a tote bag that is used only for your writing time, and keep your supplies in it.

EXERCISES

Step 1. Look over your week's schedule and your time blocks. Schedule an appointment with yourself for an available time. Write it down as many places as possible.

_____

_____

_____

_____

_____

_____

_____

_____

_____

_____

_____

_____

_____

_____

_____

Step 2. Create your writer's tote bag and binder. Make the checklist of things you will need to bring with you. Put this checklist on the front of your binder.

_____

_____

_____

_____

_____

_____

_____

_____

_____

_____

_____

_____

_____

_____

_____

_____

_____

_____

_____

14. CREATE A TO-DO LIST

Creating a to-do list at the beginning of each day with the tasks you intend to accomplish can help to ensure that you are making daily progress in the right direction. However, many people make to-do lists that are unrealistic and end up being the whip they use to flog themselves for failure as a result. Here are a few things to remember when creating a to-do list for your day.

Keep It Short

The shorter your to-do list, the easier it is to accomplish everything that needs to be done. You should have no more than three to five items on your to-do list. Beside each task on your to-do list write down the date by which it must be completed. This way, if something should later come up that must be added to your list, you can prioritize everything appropriately. Every day your to-do list should incorporate forward progress on your writing goal to the extent that your time allows.

Write It Down

It's tempting to tell yourself that you will remember, but relying on your memory to prompt you is a recipe for forgetting things. Furthermore, anything you do with your body helps to reinforce the memory and ingrain it a little deeper in your brain. Lastly, writing it down allows you to visibly track the progress you are making toward achieving your goals.

Check It Off

Once you have completed a task, checking it off gives you an emotional reward which will encourage you to continue making progress. Being able to check another item off your list is a small success in life, which shows you that you can succeed

81

and encourages you to try setting the bar higher the next time. It is these small, daily successes that build the confidence you need to try for bigger successes in life.

Carry It Over

Once it has been placed on your to-do list, don't remove it until it is done. If necessary, carry it over to the next day. If, however, it has been on your to-do list for a month and it still isn't done, it's time to evaluate why this item isn't being completed. This is especially true if it is your writing that is being carried over and is left undone. Is this item being carried over because you are adding too much to your to-do list for the amount of time that you have available? Is there something else you can eliminate to make the time you need?

EXERCISES

Step 1. At the beginning of each morning, create a to-do list in your time journal.

Step 2. At the end of each day, see how much you have managed to accomplish.

15. DEVELOPING DISCIPLINE

By setting appointments with yourself for when you will write and how much you will write, and then keeping those appointments and making those word count goals, you begin to develop the habits of discipline. It's these same habits that will set you apart from other writers, increase your productivity, and allow you to become the kind of writer publishing companies love having on their team.

If you want to write, you're going to have to develop the discipline needed to write. Learning to manage your time effectively is about developing the habit of saying no to some things – even things that aren't bad for you – so that you can say yes to better things, such as your writing. It takes a lot of discipline to write when everyone else in the household is playing games or goofing off.

It takes a lot of discipline to write when you're bone tired but you know you haven't hit your writing goal for the day so you stay up and write it anyway. It takes discipline to keep writing when you've faced your first or your hundredth rejection and you're wondering why you are writing this stuff anyway. Discipline is one of the main differences between someone who dreams of writing and someone who is a writer.

Publishers and Deadlines

Once you've written your book and found your publisher, you will enter the world of deadlines. Publishing houses have paychecks to pay, which means they must push their writers to meet deadlines that allow them to make those paychecks in a timely manner. The worst nightmare any editor has is an author who cannot meet deadlines. Editors have been fired because they could not get the writer assigned to them to produce their material on time.

There's so much money and time invested in marketing for a release date that every time the date is pushed back, it represents hundreds of thousands of dollars in lost revenue. This is one reason why publishing houses are reluctant to take on unproven authors. They know most of them don't have the discipline developed to meet the deadlines, and they can't afford the risks. By developing this discipline before you make it big, you will be miles ahead of other authors clamoring for the attention of the publishing world because you will be able to produce work in a timely manner.

Future Fans are Counting on You

It's not just the publishing houses that lose out when you can't meet deadlines, either. Your fans do, too. Every time you make them a promise on when you're going to deliver the content, and then you fail, you lose a little bit of their trust in you. You also lose some of your marketing momentum with each date you push back the arrival of your product and it costs you more money to make up for what you've lost. Your lack of discipline will end up meaning you produce fewer books and have fewer streams of revenue.

Don't Let Small Failures Become Permanent Defeats

When I talk about developing discipline, I want you to understand that it will not come all at once. Like a child learning to walk, you may fail to keep your appointment with yourself many times before the discipline is developed that ensures you can keep that appointment all the time, every time. Failure is a temporary setback, not a permanent defeat – unless you allow it to become permanent by not trying again. So, if you fail to make that appointment, don't give up and don't start talking badly about yourself. Examine what happened, why you failed, and learn from it so you don't have to repeat that lesson.

When You Least Feel Like Doing It, Do It Anyway

Here's something I have learned along the way: it is those days when you least feel like keeping that appointment that the greatest rewards come for keeping it. There is a negative force that doesn't want your success and that would give anything to keep you from it. That negative force likes to see you fail because it knows that when you fail, you start feeling bad about yourself and you'll feed it your negative energy. Do not give in to it! Go to your appointment and know that something incredible is going to come out of this session because you did.

Daily Decisions Develop Discipline

It is the daily decisions to keep your appointment to write when you don't feel like it, when you're tired, when you're busy, when you can't think of anything to write that develops the discipline that eventually leads to your writing success. Anyone **can** write a book, but only those who discipline themselves to write every day succeed.

EXERCISES

Step 1. Keep your appointments with yourself for the next 30 days.

Step 2. At the end of each appointment, note how you feel before you go to the appointment and how you feel after you keep the appointment.

16. ELIMINATING DISTRACTIONS

The creative brain tends to be easily distracted. This is because creative brains remain open to every source of stimuli that's around them, constantly taking things in and rarely turning the valve to the "off" position. This means that when you sit down to write, you naturally have a harder time focusing on what you are doing than anyone else in the room. That's why it's super important for you to eliminate as many distractions as you can when it comes time to actually writing.

Disconnect from the Internet

The internet is a glorious thing, very useful for research, and for connecting with others. However, during your writing appointment time, shut it off. If you're writing on a laptop, go to a place where you do not have internet access to write. If you're writing on a desktop, disconnect it until you're done if possible. This may sound harsh, but you will never be able to focus on delivering the story inside of you if you're "multi-tasking" and doing a million things at once.

The Multi-Tasking Myth

There is a myth that says the human brain can multi-task and do it well. This isn't actually true. Our brains just aren't wired that way. What happens, instead, is that we switch between tasks so rapidly that we're not really able to focus on any one of them. Details get missed and overlooked, things get forgotten, and very little actually gets done. Do not think you can do a million tasks all at the same time and produce the same quality and quantity of writing as someone who focuses will. It won't happen.

A Quiet Space

Quiet spaces really are the best places to work and, especially, to write. The quiet allows you to focus on what you are doing. If there is no quiet space at home, try the library, a coffee shop, or even a cemetery if it has an open park bench. Another great place to get away from all the noise and the activity is your car, especially if you are using a laptop, mobile phone, or old fashioned pen and paper to write. Drive out to a deserted place and sit in your car and write. As a Catholic, I can say with honesty that some of my best writing has come during Eucharistic Adoration when it's just me, the silence, and Jesus. The point is to find a place where you can write that eliminates as many distractions as you possibly can so you can focus your full attention on writing.

The One Exception: Music

If you need music, use classical music or strictly instrumental music so that you are neither distracted nor unduly influenced by the words. Baroque classical music such as Beethoven, Vivaldi, Mozart, or Bach is great for helping the brain relax which allows it to concentrate better on the task at hand. If you aren't keen on classical music, the target is to find strictly instrumental music, preferably at 60 beats per minute (the average pulse rate). This will keep your brain awake, alert, and active.

EXERCISES

Step 1. Choose a place for your writing appointments. Include the location in your appointment calendars and when you write it down.

Step 2. Write down the steps you are planning to take to eliminate distractions, aside from choosing the right location. Will you turn off the internet and turn on the music? Will you drop the kids off at the in-laws or hire a sitter?

_____

_____

_____

_____

_____

_____

_____

_____

_____

_____

_____

_____

_____

_____

SECTION 5:

AVOIDING THE WRITE OBSTACLES

17. TIME SINKS & TIME WASTERS

Maximizing your time is partly about learning to get more things done in less time. To do this, you have to evaluate your work habits for time sinks and time wasters. These are the things that drain your productivity and cause tasks to take even longer than they normally should. If you can eliminate as many of these as possible, you'll be able to get more done in less time than you ever imagined possible.

Plan Your Writing Time

You can get a lot more done during your writing appointment if you know what you're going to be writing before you get there. This means taking the time to outline not just the chapter headings but what goes into each chapter as well. It may feel unnatural to outline when writing fiction, but taking the time to outline each chapter's events, to visualize it and then write it out without the dialogue and details, will really help you by allowing you to play the scene in your mind several times over as you are writing, grabbing the details that come to mind.

It will also improve your writing by allowing you to pinpoint areas that actively bore you in the scene, helping you to locate areas that draw your attention and cause you to want to stay in the scene longer. Whether you are writing fiction or non-fiction, you will get more out of your writing time by taking the time to get your outline down on paper before you start.

Keep Research Time Separate

Don't research in the middle of your writing time. If you need to, set aside one writing block to devote to any research you may need to do for your upcoming writing and then bring that research with you to your writing appointment. Trying to research during your writing time will take the focus off your creative writing and can easily open your mind up to other distractions. Furthermore, switching between tasks has been actively shown to waste anywhere between three and five minutes as the brain tries to refocus on the new task.

Checking Email

Compulsive email checking is a problem for a lot of people. Put away your smart phone (unless you are using it to write), shut down your email client, and make a firm commitment that you will not check your email during your writing time. If you can, turn off the sounds that notify you when an email has been sent so that your mind isn't called back to it. Trust me, anything that's in your inbox can and will wait until you have finished. Furthermore, waiting until you are finished will give you the ability to devote your entire attention to it, with better results for you and the recipient.

EXERCISES

Step 1: What time sinks and time wasters are your biggest temptation? If you've been keeping your journal up-to-date, take a look at where you spend your time and note how often you are switching tasks, checking email, spending writing time on research, or losing valuable time because you didn't plan ahead.

Step 2: Write your plan for how you are going to reduce or eliminate these time sinks and time wasters from your schedule. What will you gain in your writing by doing this?

_____

_____

18. ORGANIZING YOUR WORK SPACE

While I already knew that organizing your work space was an important part of making the most of your time, I was confronted with the reality of how important it was just the other day. I literally spent four hours searching for a file I needed for an assignment.

What should have taken me only an hour to complete ended up taking the majority of my work day and all because I hadn't filed one item in the right place. When you keep your time journal, you will be surprised to see just how much time disorganization can cost you. Your time is too valuable to waste.

Organizing the Easy Way

One of the reasons that we don't organize is that we tell ourselves we don't have the time to get it done, but imagine if you are losing your writing time every day because you are hunting for the tools you need to get the writing done! Now, if you're like me and you've allowed things to go disorganized for a while it can take quite a bit of effort to get things cleaned up and in order.

However, this doesn't mean you shouldn't do it. It means you need to do it in stages. Remember: You eat the elephant one bite at a time, and you organize your work space the same way. If you spend 15 minutes of every day on organizing things, you will soon find that everything is neat and tidy and then it's just a matter of maintaining the order you've created.

Find a Home

Every item you use should have a specific location for it. You store pots and pans in the kitchen, for example, because that's where you do the cooking. Storing them in the bedroom would be annoying because you'd end up having to go back and forth to the bedroom too often. Consider the best place to put each item in your home, and then stick to it. If it's something you need often, make sure it's easy to access. Don't store frequently used items on the top shelf, unless you are a very tall person and you live alone.

Play Detective

When you look at your home, where does clutter tend to accumulate the most? Find out why, and solve the problem. For example, in our house the clutter tends to accumulate on the dining room table because that's where my husband and I run our business, so everything we need gets piled up there and the piles grow high pretty quickly. We've learned to tackle that problem by purchasing a small rolling cart with three drawers that we can keep under the table so we have more room to work.

De-Clutter

Go through the clutter. Get rid of as much of it as you can. You'll be surprised at how much stuff accumulates after just a month, and most of it isn't things that you really need. If you're holding on to things for sentimental value, look through them and ask yourself whether you really need them all. See if you can't pare down your collection to one or two items.

EXERCISES

Step 1. As you are going through your things, ask yourself the following three questions: Why am I keeping this? How often do I use it? Do I really need it? Why do I need it?

Step 2. Look over your time journal. How often do you lose time to the clutter? How much time could you find for your writing if you were to organize your house or writing space?

_____

_____

_____

_____

_____

_____

_____

_____

_____

_____

_____

_____

19. THE FINE ART OF SAYING "NO"

This chapter most often applies to women far more than men, but even men can have trouble establishing firm boundaries and learning to say "no". Women are taught early on that saying "no" can hurt other people's feelings, so they tend to avoid it at all cost in the mistaken belief that saying "yes" is the "nice" thing to do.

The Truth About Setting Boundaries

Boundaries are part of any healthy relationship, and you need to learn to set them. When you say yes to things you don't want to do because you're afraid of hurting someone else's feelings, you aren't being honest with that person about what matters to you. That kind of deception is no foundation for a relationship of any kind and, because you are saying yes when you'd rather say no, you will only end up resenting them for the fact that you are doing something you'd rather not do. An honest "no" is far better than a reluctant "yes" any day.

You Are a Finite Being

Although there have been some Catholic saints who have been able to bilocate (be in two places at one time), few of us are granted that privilege. Most of us must content ourselves with having to choose between activities, especially activities that take place at the same time or in very different locations. You must learn to accept the fact that you cannot accomplish everything in life. You must learn to say "no" to some things so that you can give a full and hearty "yes" to everything that you agree to do.

Use Your Schedule to Your Advantage

Now that you know what your schedule actually looks like, when you are asked to take on any new project tell the person you must first consult your calendar. Look it over. Do you have the time to add this project AND still get your writing done? Will this activity take away from time with your family or friends? Will it conflict with an existing commitment?

Does this new activity support your primary or secondary goals in life? If you can answer no to any of these questions, explain to the person who asked you that you checked your calendar and there simply isn't sufficient time for you to devote to the project and still do a good job.

Don't Make Excuses

If you don't want to do something or don't have time to do it, say so openly and honestly. Don't hide behind lame excuses. These insult the intelligence of the person asking you and are actually more hurtful than the honesty would be. Furthermore, because you aren't being honest, it leaves them with the impression that you will say yes once certain conditions have been met. You don't really want to do this at all, but you're giving false hope to someone by implying that you will later on. Don't leave that door open by trying to "let someone down gently." Rather, be direct and forthright about why you aren't willing to do something.

The Necessity of Saying "No" to Good Things

Even a project that is worthy of being done, like charity or volunteer work, should not always be given a yes. After all, if you are so busy that saying yes to these things would require you to neglect your prayer/meditation time or would require you to give up large amounts of time with your family in order to do them, they are a distraction and are not going to bring the fruit that they would otherwise. If something, however noble it might seem, leaves you with no time for being with the most important people in your life, then you should probably re-evaluate its place in your life.

EXERCISES

Step 1. Do you have trouble saying "no"? Why? Do you know someone who has trouble saying no? What has been the consequences of his or her decision to say "yes" when they didn't want to say "yes"? Is this an example you want to follow?

_____

_____

_____

_____

_____

_____

_____

_____

Step 2. Practice saying no, without apology, when you don't want to do things.

20. COMMIT TO EXCELLENCE

If you don't have time to do it, you definitely don't have time to do it twice. When you accept a project or put something on your to-do list, especially when that something is your writing, you need to be able to make a commitment that you will give it your best effort.

If you look over your schedule and you see that there is no way you can devote the amount of time it will take to produce your absolute best work, to commit to excellence, then you have no business saying "yes" to that assignment or that project. This policy will not only protect your reputation as an author and a worker but will also ensure that you do not overload your plate with projects to the point where you are delivering poor quality goods because you don't have the time to devote to the work.

What Your Quality of Work Says About You

Especially as an author, the quality of your work speaks to your character. The care you take when crafting your writing and the dedication you show in ensuring that your product is as error free as you could possibly make it before you release it into the wild will tell the people who read your work something about you.

If you always strive for high quality work, if your work is always as excellent as you can make it, you will earn people's trust and they will be willing to devote their time to reading more of what you write because you are showing them by how you work that you respect their time and appreciate their attention. It also shows that you believe in yourself, and that you are the kind of person who never gives anything less than your personal best. It shows that you have a serious commitment to your craft, and that you respect both the time of the readers and your own time.

Someone who produces shoddy work, whose attention to detail is poor and who puts no effort into finding and correcting errors, by contrast shows a total disrespect for the time and commitment of the people who read it, as well as a lack of self-respect. A few people may be fooled into buying copies of the poorly produced work, but most people are not going to bother coming back for more. Take pride in your writing because it is your ambassador to the world.

Excellence vs. Perfectionism

A commitment to excellence is not the same thing as seeking perfection. Striving for excellence demands that you give it your very best effort. Notice that the focus here is on the effort given and not on the results produced. Perfectionism focuses on the results while ignoring the effort to get those results. Perfectionism sets you up for failure because you are not perfect and cannot achieve that goal. You can only do your best.

The Dangers of Perfectionism

Perfectionism hampers the progress you make toward your writing goal by rejecting everything you produce as "not good enough." It focuses only on the flaws, the things that are wrong, and defeats you. A perfectionist will put something on the to-do list and never end up taking it off or marking it as finished because there is always "one more change" that could be made to improve it.

If you allow perfectionism to take over the creative process, you could spend years and years and years writing without ever reaping any reward, become discouraged, and ultimately give up on your dream. This is why I speak so urgently that you are not to seek perfection in your work, but excellence. Let your quest for excellence, however, be unwavering.

Excellence Demands Attention

You cannot produce excellent work while distracted. The better able you are to focus your attention on what you are doing, the higher quality of work that you will produce. This is another reason to do everything you can to eliminate as many distractions as you possibly can while writing, to get all the rest you need and the right kinds of foods so that you can truly focus your attention where you need it. This will allow you to pay attention to the details, and it is those details that are the difference between the master work and the work of an amateur.

Get Others to Review Your Work

Once, I was painting an ocean scene from my imagination. I knew something was missing, but I was tempted to leave it that way because I didn't quite know what that something was.

However, I decided instead to ask my husband for his input. Immediately he pointed to a spot on the painting that was just too open and empty - the negative space there was overpowering and it was drawing attention away from the rest of the scene. With a few brush strokes, I added in a tiny island jutting slightly from the side of the painting which broke up the negative space and returned the focus to the ship in the center. The painting was now exactly right, and I must admit to this day it is one of my favorites, all because I stopped to ask for other eyes to help me look things over.

You are often too close to your work to accurately judge how good it is. This is why your pursuit of excellence requires you to find other eyes to help review your work. A fresh pair of eyes can spot inconsistencies and problems with your work, and can even sometimes point out solutions you hadn't thought of that will help you break through and push forward. This is especially true in your writing, as your mind often assumes it knows what is written on the page and will overlook errors that someone else can easily detect.

EXERCISES

Step 1. Evaluate where you are in terms of your commitment to excellence. Are you taking on too many projects without first checking to be sure you have the time to properly devote to them? Do you fall into the trap of perfectionism, constantly making changes and never moving the project off of your to-do list because of it? What can you do to change things if you need to change them?

_____

_____

_____

_____

_____

_____

_____

_____

_____

Step 2. Write out an action plan for ensuring that every project, including your writing, gets the time and attention it needs to be excellent.

_____

_____

_____

_____

_____

_____

_____

_____

_____

_____

_____

_____

_____

_____

Step 3. Write out what standards your projects must meet to be considered "excellent" by you. Keep this checklist for excellence close at hand and use it for every piece of work you undertake.

_____

_____

_____

_____

_____

_____

_____

_____

_____

_____

_____

_____

_____

_____

Section 6:

Staying on The Write Path

21. MANAGING MULTIPLE DEADLINES

Managing multiple deadlines is a skill that is a necessity for most writers at some point in their career. A typical example is that you may be maintaining a blog while you're writing a manuscript while you are also guest blogging for someone else, and the content needs to be produced in a timely manner just to maintain and grow the audience you've built. It's a skill that most people need at some point regardless of where they are in life. Here are some strategies I've learned during my years as a secretary for managing multiple deadlines.

First Due, First Done

It may seem obvious, but sometimes the project that's due first is one we don't want to work on to begin with and so we push it to the side until it's just about late. Adopt a policy of first due, first done and you'll solve more than half of your problems in managing multiple deadlines. If you need to still show progress on your other projects, this is where you go straight back to your time blocks and rearrange them so that the lion's share of time is devoted to whatever is due out first but there is still some time allocated to your other tasks.

Competing Deadlines

There are times when you may have projects due at the same time. This doesn't mean you need to panic, but it does mean you need to examine both projects carefully. Is there one that will be faster for you to complete? Do that one first and get it out of the way so that you can devote the majority of your time to the more difficult project. If both projects are going to require the same amount of effort to complete, decide whether or not both projects actually need to be done. If they do, it's time to delegate, delay, or schedule the projects.

113

Delegate, Delay, or Schedule

If possible, delay one of the projects until a later date. If you can't delay it, see if you can delegate the task to someone else. This may involve hiring a ghost writer to handle your blog posts for a week, or an accountant to take care of your taxes so you can focus on the project that really matters to you. If you cannot delegate the task or delay it until later, schedule time to devote to both projects. You may have to rearrange your other scheduled tasks but if it's truly important, it's worth devoting the time to doing it. Work on both projects a little at a time until they are both completed.

Get Help

When you've got multiple projects that you can't drop, you can't delay, and you can't delegate the whole thing, see if there isn't some part of it that you can delegate. Maybe, for example, you can't afford to hire a ghost writer – can you find a guest blogger for a couple of days a week? If at least some part of the project is being handled by someone else, this can free up your time to devote to the writing you really enjoy.

EXERCISES

Step 1. What is your current strategy for managing multiple deadlines? How is it working for you?

_____

_____

_____

_____

Step 2. What can you do to improve how you are currently handling it? What can you delay? What can you delegate? What can you schedule?

_____

_____

_____

Step 3. What would happen if you failed to meet your deadlines? What are the costs involved? Who would be most hurt by your failure? Do these things truly align with your biggest priorities?

_____

_____

_____

_____

_____

_____

_____

22. HANDLING PROCRASTINATION

Vic Johnson, a mentor of mine, once stated that the largest nation on earth was Procrasti-nation. It's true. Most people spend their lives procrastinating on tasks they need or even want to do, and they never bother to figure out why they do this. It's actually kind of insane, if you think about it, because we do this even on matters where the result of failure could end up in the loss of the very things that matter most to us – our homes, our families, our careers!

The Procrastination Game

Procrastination is not as much of a challenge for me as it used to be, but this is in large part because I figured out why I was procrastinating in the first place. I love to have fun. I will often turn boring tasks into games in order to make them less boring for me to do, and without consciously realizing that is exactly what I was doing with my procrastination. It turned boring tasks, tasks I didn't really want to do or wasn't sure I could do, into an exciting game.

Suddenly, instead of just having to do taxes, I was having to race against the clock to see if I could assemble everything and get it all completed in time to drop it off at the post office before the clock struck midnight. It injected a bit of drama into an otherwise dull task. I have since learned how to turn these boring tasks into a game without procrastinating. For the taxes, as an example, I race to see how quickly I can finish them instead of allowing the deadline to arrive with me unprepared.

Reasons For Procrastination

Most of us procrastinate for one of four simple reasons: we don't know how to do what we're supposed to do, we don't

117

understand what we are supposed to do, we are concerned we can't do what we've been asked to do, or the task is so easy for us that it is boring. Of course, there are really simple solutions to all of these reasons and none of them involves putting them off another day or another week. Procrastination never makes your life easier, it actually ends up making it more difficult.

If you don't know how to do what it is you need to do, go ahead and find someone who has done it and ask them what needs to be done. I put off formatting this book for two weeks because even though I knew older versions of Word quite well I didn't know the particular version I was using well enough to know how to get it done. However, I finally decided that I was just going to sit down and flip through all the features and figure it out. I spent two hours of time playing with the software, got everything figured out, and finished the manuscript in a single evening.

If you don't understand what it is you're supposed to do, keep asking until you find someone who can explain it to you. There's nothing wrong with not understanding something, even if someone has explained it to you before. Ask them to go over it again, or find someone who will if they won't.

If your fear is that you can't do it, or you're overwhelmed by the amount there is to do, this next section is especially for you.

Break It Down

All big projects are actually a series of small projects that come together to form a larger project. So, to reduce the feeling of being overwhelmed and to make the project more manageable, break it down into its components. This will also help you to figure out which parts of the task can be delegated to someone else. Sit down with a notepad and pen and brainstorm what the first step would be to complete your task.

Then ask yourself what task comes next, and keep following through until you have a plan.

Just as a staircase, no matter how tall, is climbed just one step at a time so any task that you face can be accomplished if you can first find one step to take. Don't write it off as impossible. Picture your success, and then imagine how you got there.

EXERCISES

Step 1. Identify the tasks you have been procrastinating on the most.

Step 2. Go over each task. Why have you been procrastinating in getting them done? What steps will it take to get this done?

Step 3. Write out an action plan for what you are going to do – specifically – to handle getting these tasks off your to-do list.

_____

_____

_____

_____

_____

_____

_____

_____

BRANDY M. MILLER

23. ACCOUNTABILITY PARTNERS

Along with your time journal, you should find a few close friends or family members who are willing to hold your feet to the fire in terms of making the most of your time and reaching your goals. This is because when it's just you looking at things, it becomes easy to rationalize quitting on your dreams and shoving them to the back burner for the eleventy-billionth time (yes, I know – not a real word). However, when there are other people who know your dreams and who are committed to your success because they truly love you and care about you and want what is best for you – they won't allow you to slide behind the curtain of excuses and hide your talents from the world forever. They will hold you accountable for your success.

Accept Constructive Criticism

Before you seek out accountability partners, you need to be honest about your ability to accept constructive criticism and take helpful admonishment. If you aren't willing to change, or you don't take these things well, there's no point in doing the work it will take to find an accountability partner. You'll waste both your time and your partner's, and create resentment between the two of you. Remember that these people are actively working for your greater good because they really care about you and not because they want to hurt you, oppress you, or control you. So, put aside your ego and open yourself up to let them in because the results will be worth it.

The Ideal Partner

Not everyone is suited to be an accountability partner. Some people are too negative in their beliefs. If they don't believe that your goals are achievable, if they don't have dreams of their own they are working toward, they are not a suitable candidate. You need someone with the ability to believe in you when you have lost sight of hope for yourself. These people have to be

121

die hard positive batteries who can help you recharge your own when you are feeling completely drained. They need to be people who are cheerleaders who won't quit on you and won't let you quit on you, either.

However, they also need to be people who are problem solvers and can help you figure out a solution for your obstacles rather than just telling you to get over them or move past them. If you can't find someone, I will help you. You can find my Facebook fan page (https://www.facebook.com/pages/The-Write-Time/369626579821437) or contact me at my website (http://40daywriter.com). I know you can do great things, and I want you to do them because the world needs you to do them.

Regular Meetings

When you find your accountability partner or partners, meet with them regularly for a time usage "check-up". Bring your time journal with you so that you can go over things with them and they can help you spot trends you haven't spotted in your time management behaviors. This isn't a mentor-mentee situation. You should be offering to help them as well, so that neither of you is gaining at the expense of the other. Invite them to join with you and to allow you to review their time journal, too.

EXERCISES

Step 1. Who do you know already who might be willing to be an accountability partner for you? Do they meet the ideal requirements?

Step 2. Reach out online. See if you can't find a group that already exists, a forum or message board, or a Facebook friend that you can turn to for help.

Step 3. Write down an action plan of how the two of you are going to meet and hold each other accountable for proper time management.

_____

_____

_____

_____

_____

_____

_____

_____

_____

_____

_____

24. BUILDING IN "YOU" TIME

Your life cannot be all about work, school, or even all about your writing. There must be some time for you to be you. You need some time to get away from everything, some time to relax and enjoy your life, and some time to decompress. The brain needs these breaks, even from writing. Your writing will improve because these breaks will give you new experiences and bring to mind new ideas that you can then add to your collection of things to pull from when you are writing. Furthermore, these experiences may well provide the inspiration for whole new stories – especially when interacting with new people.

Schedule Reward Times

Make down times your reward for having achieved your goals each day or each week. When you see you've hit that mark, celebrate by taking a little time to yourself. If you finished a task sooner than you expected, reward yourself and take the rest of the time for yourself. Read a good book, take a walk, enjoy time with your friends or family, or play that video game you've been putting off. Set a timer if you need to so you can get back to your schedule once you're done, but just be in the moment and enjoy it.

Take One Day a Week Off

Take one day a week off to rest your mind and your body from the rest of the week's work. Use that day to nurture and grow your relationships with other people. Spend time on social media pages, attend or invite people for a family dinner, go to the movies or just hang out with friends. Don't write, and don't think about writing. Let your mind be in the moment and enjoy what's right there in front of you. It will recharge your mental batteries and allow you to be refreshed, ready to conquer and do more the following week.

Fun Is Important

Fun keeps depression, boredom, and negative emotions at bay, so be sure to build in some fun time during your "me" time. If you didn't have much of a childhood because of the chaos in your household, there's no time like the present to learn how. Do something silly and spontaneous simply because you want to without worrying about what others will think.

Follow an impulse and see where it leads you (provided the impulse isn't to do something that would harm yourself or others). Want to take a drive? Gas up the car and go! See where the road takes you. Explore your world. There's plenty of it, and you only have one life to do it in, so now's as good a time as any. Besides, everything you see, hear, taste, touch, or smell is one more thing you can add to your writing experiences pot.

EXERCISES

Step 1. Look at your time blocks. Which day will work best for your day off if you don't already have one?

_____

_____

_____

_____

Step 2. Go have fun!

126

WHAT DID YOU THINK?

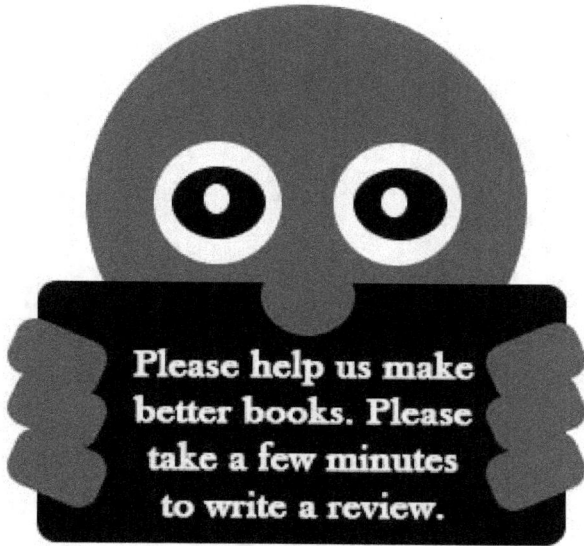

Please help us make better books. Please take a few minutes to write a review.

Special Offer:

Visit 40 Day Writer (http://40daywriter.com) & subscribe to our mailing list for a FREE 120 day time journal in PDF format which you can download & print out. PLUS you'll be the first to know about webinars, special events, upcoming books & book signings.

About the Author

Brandy M. Miller has been writing since she was very young, although this is only her third book in print. She studied Graphic Design and, later, Game Art and Design through the Art Institute Online. She obtained an Associates Degree in Elementary Education from the Gillette Campus of Sheridan College in Gillette, Wyoming.

She currently works as a Creativity Consultant for Creative Technology Services (http://nvcreativetechnology.com), a company she and her husband started together in November of 2011. She sees her job as helping people to tap into their own creative energy in order to solve real-world problems. She also operates 40 Day Writer (http://40daywriter.com), a website dedicated to helping aspiring authors find the success they desire. She is also the current President of the Elko County Art Club (http://elkocountyartclub.org), and a founding member of Elko County Writers (http://elkocountywriters.org). Elko County Writers exists to help foster friendship and professional growth for writers living in Elko County.

She lives in Elko, Nevada with her husband and son. Her hobbies include painting, drawing, writing, reading, sewing and designing fabrics, and playing video games. Her favorite television shows are NCIS, Bones, Grimm, Castle, and Touch. She is neither Republican nor Democrat, she is quite happily Catholic and votes accordingly.

Connect with her online:

Twitter: http://twitter.com/WriterBrandy

Facebook: https://www.facebook.com/pages/The-Write-Time/369626579821437

LinkedIn: www.linkedin.com/in/brandymmiller/

Blog: http://brandy-miller.blogspot.com

Business Website: http://nvcreativetechnology.com

40 Day Writer: http://40daywriter.com

Elko County Writers: http://elkocountywriters.org

Elko County Art Club: http://elkocountyartclub.org